Contents

How to Teach Nonfiction Writing • EMC 719

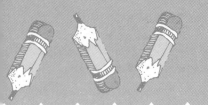

Part I
Introduction

You write nonfiction whenever you write about real-life experiences—when you write about what is true and accurate. You are writing nonfiction when you…

- write a letter to a friend
- record observations during a science experiment
- write directions to your house for a friend
- complete invitations to a party
- list the steps for a recipe
- send a letter of complaint to a business
- write a report

Be alert to naturally occurring occasions within the classroom that lend themselves to writing nonfiction. Page 3 provides some ideas.

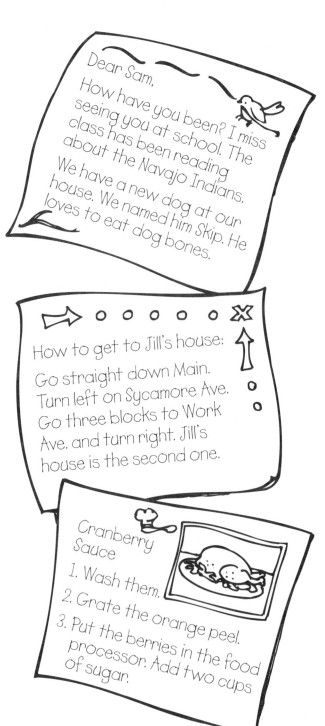

Dear Sam,
How have you been? I miss seeing you at school. The class has been reading about the Navajo Indians. We have a new dog at our house. We named him Skip. He loves to eat dog bones.

How to get to Jill's house:
Go straight down Main. Turn left on Sycamore Ave. Go three blocks to Work Ave. and turn right. Jill's house is the second one.

Cranberry Sauce
1. Wash them.
2. Grate the orange peel.
3. Put the berries in the food processor. Add two cups of sugar.

How to Teach Nonfiction Writing • EMC 719

Writing Nonfiction Across the Curriculum

Language Arts/Reading
- keep daily logs of assigned and self-selected literature being read
- keep reading logs in various subject areas: social studies, science, etc.
- write authentic stories to express feelings and share information

Social Studies
- write reports of various lengths; include graphic components
- write biographical sketches about historical people and people currently in the news
- write essays about places and events, both historical and current
- write to public officials regarding a concern about the community or country

Science
- record observations of science experiments
- record observations made while raising a plant or an animal
- record observations made on field trips
- write about an element of science, an important scientific discovery, or a scientist

Math
- write a step-by-step explanation of how a problem was solved
- write a paragraph explaining the meaning of a math symbol
- list ten ways math is used in your life

Physical Education
- explain the rules and playing strategies for a game
- write a descriptive paragraph explaining how it feels to play/win/lose a game
- write a report or create a picture book about a favorite sports figure

Art and Music
- write a biographical sketch of a famous artist
- explain how a certain medium or technique is used
- describe a favorite form of artistic expression and explain why it is a favorite

Health
- give the recipe for preparing a healthy dish
- list all of the foods eaten for one day, explaining how each fits into the food pyramid
- explain why one of the following is important for good health–sleep, nutritious food, exercise

The Writing Process

Prewriting—Prewriting is what the writer does before writing begins. It's the time to motivate and collect words, thoughts, facts, and questions to use when writing. This step draws on the writer's experiences.

Prewriting is the time to:

- review steps in the writing format to be used
- brainstorm possible topics
- discuss the intended audience
- determine the focus of the piece
- organize ideas and collect information

Drafting—This is the writer's first expression of ideas in written form. The writer takes ideas and information and writes a rough draft.

- Beginning—Grab the attention of the reader and introduce the subject.
- Middle—Provide facts and examples to support or clarify the subject.
- Conclusion—Summarize the main ideas of the piece and remind the reader why the subject is memorable or important.

Responding—The writer rereads the piece to make sure that it makes sense. The writer shares it to get responses from others. (See page 5 for more information.)

page 5

Revising—The writer changes the rough draft to state ideas more clearly. This is the time to look at phrases and words that express the writer's ideas in a more precise and interesting way. (See page 6 for a revising and editing checklist.)

Editing—This is the point at which the writer checks the mechanics such as grammar, punctuation, and spelling. (See page 6 for a revising and editing checklist.)

page 6

Rewriting—The writer rewrites to include all the changes made during revising and editing.

Publishing—The writer presents the final story in a finished form. It is shared with others in some way. This sharing with others is a motivating factor for students, as well as an important element in the writing process.

Responding to Writing

Modeling the Process

Before students work in response pairs or small groups, the response process should be carefully modeled. If necessary, spend a number of weeks being the responder to student writing. Be clear about what facets of writing you are responding to (sentence structure, use of adjectives, clarity of ideas, etc.) so that students become aware of the scope of appropriate responses.

Important Guidelines

- Responses should be respectful.

- Responses are addressed to the author.

- Responses are designed to help authors be better writers.

  "Ben, you might give more facts to show why you think that is true."

  (Not, *"I don't understand."*)

- Responses should be specific.

  "Sandy, I liked the way you explained the steps to that game."

  (Not, *"I liked your report."*)

- Responses should be sensitive.

  "Tom, I don't understand why it's important to recycle aluminum cans. Can you explain that to the reader in a more complete way?"

  (Not, *"That doesn't make sense."*)

Response Groups

- Whole class
  One student shares with the rest of the class. The class listens carefully, compliments specific parts of the writing, and asks questions for clarification or more information. You may find it helpful to limit the number of compliments and questions.

- Small group
  Groups follow the whole-class procedure.

- Partners
  Two writers work together. They take turns sharing their writings and responding with compliments and questions. A more formal response can be facilitated by having the responder fill out a response form after reading or hearing the sample. Use the form on page 7 or create your own form to address the specific skills your class is working on.

Name _____

Think about these questions as you revise and edit your writing.

Revise:

☐ Is my subject clear?

☐ Are my topic sentences and supporting details stated clearly?

☐ Do I need to add anything?

☐ Do I need to cut any parts?

☐ Do I need to change my language to make the piece more interesting or easier to understand?

☐ Do I need to put things in a different order?

☐ Will the beginning grab the reader's interest?

Edit:

☐ Have I used correct punctuation?

☐ Have I spelled everything correctly?

☐ Did I use correct grammar?

Writing Response Form

Name _____

Title of writing: _____

Date _____ Reviewer's name _____

Areas of strength: _____

_____

_____

Areas needing change: _____

_____

_____

Date _____ Reviewer's name _____

Areas of strength: _____

_____

_____

Areas needing change: _____

_____

_____

Writing Portfolios

page 9

Prepare a simple writing portfolio. Staple the contents sheet on page 9 to the inside of a sturdy folder. Attach the cover form on page 10.

Use the writing portfolios to:

- **store student writing**

  Students should date and file their writing samples. When a sample is added, it is recorded on the contents sheet.

- **generate ideas**

  Students can review samples to choose a piece they would like to develop further. Students can reread or refer to previous writing as they edit and revise current writing.

page 10

- **document student progress**

  It is valuable to compare pieces written at the beginning of the year with pieces written at the end of the year. Look at the paper with specific objectives in mind and document growth in achieving those objectives.

Individual Writing Conferences

page 7

As your students practice writing various types of nonfiction, meet with them to discuss their individual progress and possible areas for growth. Record student and teacher comments (see page 7). Attach the evaluation form to the writing sample and return it to the writing portfolio.

1. Choose a writing sample from the writing portfolio.
2. Discuss and evaluate the sample for specific skills.
3. Record strengths and areas that need improvement.
4. Develop a goal for future writing.

Portfolio Contents

Name _____

Date	Title of Piece	Comments

Writing I would like to share—expository, narrative, and persuasive. See how my writing has improved.

My Writing Portfolio

Name

How to Teach Nonfiction Writing • EMC 719

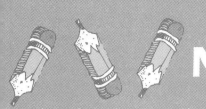 

Part II
Narrative Writing

What Is It?

Nonfiction narratives relate a true story about an event, an experience, or a person. This may be personal or biographical. Nonfiction narratives:

- relate ideas, observations, or memories
- may impart a lesson or message
- follow the elements of a good story
- use words that help make the piece come alive for the reader
- provide a reason why the experience, event, or person is memorable

Using This Section

page 12

1. Enlarge, mount, and laminate the chart on page 12. Post it on a bulletin board dedicated to nonfiction writing. Use it to introduce nonfiction narratives and refer to it as you teach the lessons in this section.

2. This section provides four personal narrative writing experiences (pages 13–19) and a lesson on writing a friendly letter (pages 20–22). Choose those appropriate to the needs of your students.

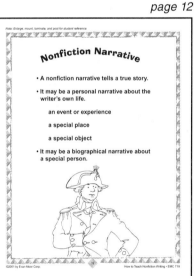

pages 14–19

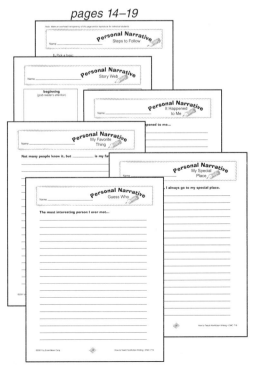

pages 21 and 22

Nonfiction Narrative

- **A nonfiction narrative tells a true story.**

- **It may be a personal narrative about the writer's own life.**

> **an event or experience**

> **a special place**

> **a special object**

- **It may be a biographical narrative about a special person.**

Writing a Personal Narrative

Students will write true stories. They may write about an event, an experience, a special place, a special object, or a memorable person.

Prepare in Advance

- "Steps to Follow" on page 14, reproduced on an overhead transparency and for individual students

- story web on page 15, reproduced for individual students

- writing form (chosen from pages 16–19), reproduced for individual students

- revise and edit checklist on page 6, reproduced for individual students

Prewriting

1. Using the information on page 14, discuss the steps students will follow as they write.

2. Provide a topic category (event, experience, place, object, or person) chosen from the forms on pages 16–19. Discuss the types of things students may write about that topic. List their ideas on a chart or chalkboard.

3. Students:

- select a topic (What do I want to write about?)

- think about their audience (Who is going to read my narrative?)

- think about the voice of the piece (Is this about something funny? Is it about a serious matter?)

4. Students make a simple story web (page 15) to serve as a guide as they write.

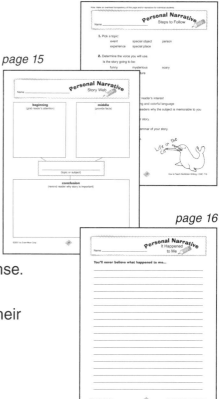

page 14

page 15

page 16

Writing

1. Using their story web, students write a rough draft.

2. Students reread the piece to make sure that it makes sense. The writer may seek another person's response.

3. Using the checklist on page 6, students revise and edit their work and recopy on another form if necessary.

Personal Narrative
Steps to Follow

Name _____

1. Pick a topic:

event   special object   person

experience   special place

2. Determine the voice you will use.

Is the story going to be:

funny   mysterious   scary

sad   a mixture

3. Complete a story web.

4. Write a rough draft.

beginning—grab your reader's interest

middle—use interesting and colorful language

conclusion—remind readers why the subject is memorable to you

5. Revise the language of your story.

6. Edit the punctuation and grammar of your story.

7. Share your story with others.

Name _____

Personal Narrative
Story Web

beginning
(grab reader's attention)

middle
(provide facts)

_____
(topic or subject)

conclusion
(remind reader why story is important)

Personal Narrative
It Happened
to Me

You'll never believe what happened to me...

_____

_____

_____

_____

_____

_____

_____

_____

_____

_____

_____

_____

_____

_____

_____

_____

Name _____

Not many people know it, but _____ **is my favorite thing.**

_____

_____

_____

_____

_____

_____

_____

_____

_____

_____

_____

_____

_____

_____

_____

_____

Personal Narrative
My Special Place

When I want to be alone, I always go to my special place.

_____

_____

_____

_____

_____

_____

_____

_____

_____

_____

_____

_____

_____

_____

_____

How to Teach Nonfiction Writing • EMC 719

Name _____

The most interesting person I ever met...

_____

_____

_____

_____

_____

_____

_____

_____

_____

_____

_____

_____

_____

_____

_____

How to Teach Nonfiction Writing • EMC 719

Writing a Friendly Letter

Friendly letters provide an opportunity to communicate what is happening in the writer's life and to ask questions about what is happening to the recipient.

Prepare in Advance

- "Friendly Letter Form" on page 21, reproduced on an overhead transparency and for individual students
- writing form on page 22, reproduced for individual students
- stationery and envelopes (optional)

Prewriting

1. Make an overhead transparency of the form on page 21. Use this to teach or review the parts of a friendly letter.

page 21

2. Brainstorm to name people to whom students might write a friendly letter. List these on a chart or chalkboard. In some instances, all students will write to the same person (e.g., a thank-you note to someone who has helped the class). Other times, individual students will select a person to write to.

Discuss the types of information students might include in a friendly letter. For example, write to a friend, pen pal, or relative describing what you are doing in school, or write a letter to someone you have read about in a periodical explaining why you admire him or her.

3. Students are assigned or select a person to write to. They think about what they wish to include in the letter.

page 22

Writing

1. Students write a rough draft using the form on page 22.

2. Students reread the piece to make sure that it makes sense. The writer may share it to get another person's response.

3. Students revise and edit their work, and then produce a final copy on stationery.

4. Students address an envelope and mail the letter.

Name _____

A Friendly Letter
Basic Form

your address

number street
city, state zip code
month day, year

date

greeting

Dear _____ ,

body of letter

indent

_____

_____

_____

_____

_____

_____

_____

_____

_____

Your Friend, **closing**

signature

_____

A Friendly Letter

Name _____

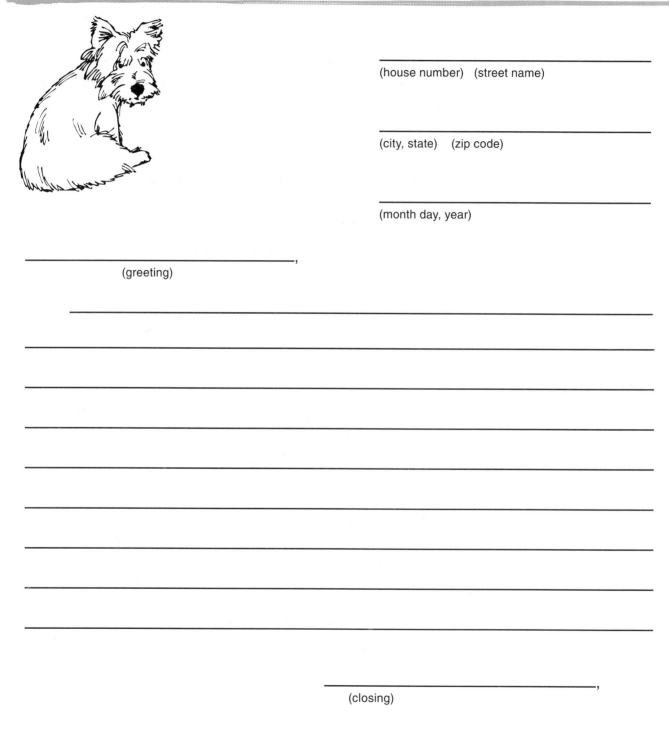

_____
(house number)   (street name)

_____
(city, state)   (zip code)

_____
(month day, year)

_____,
(greeting)

_____

_____

_____

_____

_____

_____

_____

_____

_____,
(closing)

_____
(signature)

22

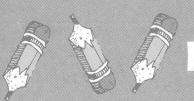

Part III
Expository Writing

What Is It?

Expository writing explains ideas, provides information, and describes "how to." Expository writing is all around us—directions for games, how to use a product, articles in a newspaper, steps in a recipe, etc. Expository writing:

- provides information

- explains ideas

- describes how to do something, how something works, how to get from one place to another

- makes comparisons (how two or more items are alike and how they are different)

- states a problem or question and provides reasonable solutions

- requires that the writer…

> develop the topic clearly
> use facts, figures, and examples to support the main idea
> write in an orderly manner (by time, place, or importance)

Using This Section

1. Enlarge, mount, and laminate the chart on page 24. Post it on a bulletin board dedicated to nonfiction writing. Use it to introduce expository writing, and refer to it as you teach the lessons in this section.

2. This section provides experiences in writing expository paragraphs that inform, explain, or compare and contrast (pages 26–30); writing a news article (pages 31–33); and writing directions (pages 34–38). Choose those appropriate to the needs of your students.

page 24

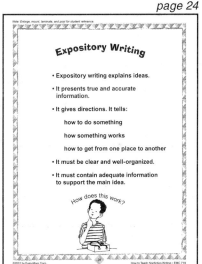

page 29

page 32

page 35

23

Expository Writing

- **Expository writing explains ideas.**

- **It presents true and accurate information.**

- **It gives directions. It tells:**

  how to do something

  how something works

  how to get from one place to another

- **It must be clear and well-organized.**

- **It must contain adequate information to support the main idea.**

How does this work?

How to Teach Nonfiction Writing • EMC 719

Name _____

Expository Writing
Steps to Follow

1. Pick a topic.

2. Think about the type of writing you will use:

• an explanation

• a news article

• directions

• an informational paragraph

3. Make an outline.

4. Write a rough draft. State the subject or main idea and provide facts and/or examples to support it.

5. Revise the language of your piece.

6. Edit the punctuation and grammar of your piece.

7. Share your writing with others.

I wish they would get their facts right. I live at the *South Pole!*

Writing Expository Paragraphs

Students will write paragraphs that inform, explain, and compare.

Prepare in Advance

- "Steps to Follow" on page 25, reproduced on an overhead transparency and for individual students
- paragraph planning sheet on page 27, reproduced for individual students
- writing form (chosen from pages 28–30), reproduced for individual students
- revise and edit checklist on page 6, reproduced for individual students

page 25

Prewriting

1. Using the chart on page 25, discuss the steps students will follow as they write.

2. Provide the topic category (informative, explanatory, or compare and contrast) chosen from the forms on pages 28–30.

Brainstorm to write a list of possible main idea sentences students might use. Discuss the types of supporting details students may write about that topic. List their ideas on a chart or chalkboard.

3. Students think about the topic and decide what they want to include. They then complete a planning form (page 27) to develop their main idea/topic sentence and supporting facts or examples.

page 27

Writing

1. Using their outlines, students write a rough draft including:

- the subject/topic of the piece
- facts and/or examples to support or illustrate the topic
- a conclusion that reviews what has been stated

2. Students reread the piece to make sure that it makes sense. The writer may seek another person's response.

3. Using the checklist on page 6, students revise and edit their work and recopy on another form if necessary.

page 29

Expository Writing
Paragraph
Planning Sheet

Name _____

Topic: _____

Type of Paragraph: _____

Main Idea: _____

_____

_____

Facts and/or Examples:

_____

_____

_____

_____

_____

_____

_____

_____

_____

_____

_____

How to Teach Nonfiction Writing • EMC 719

Expository Writing
Informing

Name _____

Recess at _____ School
(school name)

_____

_____

_____

_____

_____

_____

_____

_____

_____

_____

_____

_____

_____

_____

_____

_____

_____

Name _____

The Problem Is...

Problem: 😦

_____
_____
_____
_____
_____
_____
_____

Solution: 🙂

_____
_____
_____
_____
_____
_____
_____

Then and Now

When I was a baby _____

_____

_____

_____

_____

_____

_____

Now _____

_____

_____

_____

_____

_____

_____

Students will write a news article related to something happening in their own class, school, or community.

Prepare in Advance

- "Steps to Follow" on page 25, reproduced on an overhead transparency and for individual students
- news article planning sheet on page 32, reproduced for individual students
- writing form on page 33, reproduced for individual students
- revise and edit checklist on page 6, reproduced for individual students

Prewriting

1. Share examples of the types of articles contained in a newspaper. Analyze the elements that all good articles have in common—interesting and/or informative; accurate, up-to-date information; objective; may contain graphic elements to complete the story.

2. Brainstorm and write a list of topics students might write about. These should be topics related to the class, school, or community: a coming event, the outcome of a sports event, something special that has happened recently, or a human interest story about someone at school or in the neighborhood.

Encourage students to think of important or unusual events that will interest, inform, or entertain their readers.

page 32

page 33

3. Explain that newspaper reporters must cover all the facts about events that happen, and that they use questions to help them get all the facts.

Using the form on page 32, students will answer the following questions to outline the information for their news articles:

- Who is the story about? When did it happen?
- What happened? Why did it happen?
- Where did it happen? How did it happen?

Writing

1. Using their outlines, students write a rough draft including:

- a headline to title the piece
- an accurate telling of what happened

2. Students reread the piece to make sure that it makes sense. The writer may seek another person's response.

3. Using the checklist on page 6, students revise and edit their work and recopy on another form if necessary.

Who? _____

_____

_____

What? _____

_____

_____

Where? _____

_____

_____

When? _____

_____

_____

Why? _____

_____

_____

How? _____

_____

_____

In the News

_____
headline

_____
_____
_____
_____
_____
_____
_____
_____
_____
_____
_____
_____

Writing directions requires accuracy, attention to details, and clarity. Students can easily check how well they've done by asking someone to try to follow the directions they've written.

page 35

page 36

page 37

Prepare in Advance

- "Steps to Follow" on page 25, reproduced on an overhead transparency and for individual students

- "How to…" writing form (chosen from pages 35–38), reproduced for individual students

- revise and edit checklist on page 6, reproduced for individual students

Prewriting

1. Using the chart on page 25, review the steps students will follow as they do expository writing.

2. Select the type of directions to be written. Brainstorm to create a list of what the students should think about. List these on a chart or chalkboard.

   - Are any materials needed?
   - What steps would need to be followed?
   - In what order do you need to do each step?
   - What problems might arise?

3. Students fill in the blanks on their writing form to answer the questions posed.

Writing

1. Using the information on the planning form, students write a rough draft.

2. Students reread the piece to make sure that it makes sense. The writer may seek another person's response.

3. Students revise and edit their work and recopy on another form if necessary.

Name ________________________

Expository Writing
Game Rules

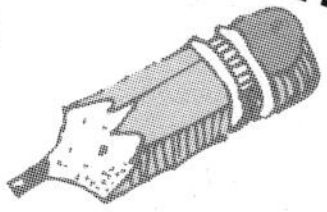

How to Play ________________________
name of game

Number of Players: ______

Equipment: ________________________

____

____

____

Rules of the Game: ________________________

____

____

____

____

____

____

____

____

Keeping Score: ____________

____

____

How do you know the winner?

____

____

Penalties (if any): ____________

____

____

Draw the playing field or game board here.

How to Cook ____

Number of Servings: _____   Cooking Temperature: _____

Ingredients: _____

_____

_____

_____   _____

_____   _____

_____   _____

Steps to Follow: _____   _____

_____   _____

_____

_____

_____

_____

_____

_____

_____

Serving Tips: _____

_____

_____

_____

Nutritional Information: _____

_____

_____

_____

How to Use a _____

Name _____

Draw a picture of the item here. Label the parts.

object

When to Use: _____

_____

_____

_____

How to Use: _____

_____

_____

_____

_____

_____

_____

Safety Tips (if needed): _____

_____

_____

_____

_____

How to Get from

Name _____

_____ **to** _____

Directions: _____

place   place

_____

_____

_____

_____

_____

_____

_____

_____

_____

_____

_____

_____

What Is It?

In persuasive writing, the writer takes a stand and supports it. The writer uses facts, figures
Draw a simple map here.

Part IV
Persuasive Writing

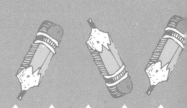

and examples in an attempt to influence the reader's thoughts or actions; to convince the reader to believe or act, as the writer wants. Persuasive writing:

- clearly states the position of the writer

- provides relevant and accurate facts and examples to support the writer's position

- anticipates and addresses reader concerns or counter arguments

Using This Section

1. Enlarge, mount, and laminate the chart on page 40. Post it on a bulletin board dedicated to nonfiction writing. Use it to introduce persuasive writing and refer to it as you teach the lessons in this section.

2. This section provides four persuasive paragraph writing experiences (pages 42–46); writing a book review (pages 47 and 48); writing a business letter (pages 49–51); and writing an editorial (pages 52 and 53). Use those appropriate to the needs of your students.

page 40

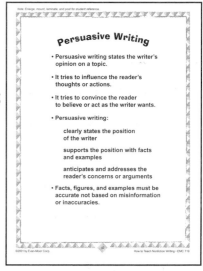

page 45

page 48

page 50

page 53

How to Teach Nonfiction Writing • EMC 719

Persuasive Writing

- **Persuasive writing states the writer's opinion on a topic.**

- **It tries to influence the reader's thoughts or actions.**

- **It tries to convince the reader to believe or act as the writer wants.**

- **Persuasive writing:**

    clearly states the position of the writer

    supports the position with facts and examples

    anticipates and addresses the reader's concerns or arguments

- **Facts, figures, and examples must be accurate, not based on misinformation or inaccuracies.**

40

Name _____

Persuasive Writing
Steps to Follow

1. State your opinion.

2. State the purpose of the piece.

3. Plan supporting details for your opinion:

   facts
   statistics
   examples
   expert opinions
   personal experience

4. Make a concluding statement.

Bananas are the best!

How to Teach Nonfiction Writing • EMC 719

Persuasive writing requires that students make good use of both language and information to convince readers to agree with the stated opinion.

Prepare in Advance

page 41

- "Steps to Follow" on page 41, reproduced on an overhead transparency and for individual students

- persuasive writing form (chosen from pages 43–46), reproduced for individual students

- revise and edit checklist on page 6, reproduced for individual students

Prewriting

1. Using the chart on page 41, discuss the steps students will follow as they do persuasive writing.

2. Provide a topic chosen from those on pages 43–46. Discuss the possible stance students may take on the topic. Brainstorm and write a list of possible arguments that might be made for or against the premise.

Writing

1. Students write a rough draft including:

- their opinion

- the purpose of the piece

- facts and/or examples to support their opinion

- a conclusion that makes one last attempt to influence the reader's opinion

2. Students reread the piece to make sure that it makes sense. The writer may seek another person's response.

3. Using the checklist on page 6, students revise and edit their work and recopy on another form if necessary.

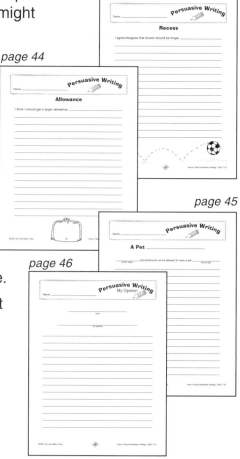

page 43

page 44

page 45

page 46

Persuasive Writing

Recess

I agree/disagree that recess should be longer. _____

_____

_____

_____

_____

_____

_____

_____

_____

_____

_____

_____

Allowance

I think I should get a larger allowance. _____

_____

_____

_____

_____

_____

_____

_____

_____

_____

_____

_____

_____

_____

A Pet _____

_____ should/should not be allowed to have a pet _____
child's name   kind of pet

_____

_____

_____

_____

_____

_____

_____

_____

_____

_____

_____

_____

_____

_____

_____

Name _____

_____
topic

_____
my opinion

_____
_____
_____
_____
_____
_____
_____
_____
_____
_____
_____
_____
_____
_____

A book review expresses the writer's understanding and opinion about a book that he or she read. The purpose of the review is to convince the reader to read or to avoid the book.

Prepare in Advance

- "Steps to Follow" on page 41, reproduced on an overhead transparency and for individual students

- book review form on page 48, reproduced for individual students

- revise and edit checklist on page 6, reproduced for individual students

Prewriting

page 41

1. Using the chart on page 41, review the steps students follow as they do persuasive writing.

2. Share several book reviews with the class. (See *The Horn Book, School Library Journal,* or *Amazon.com* for reviews.) Analyze the reviews to see what types of information are included.

3. Brainstorm and make a list of the points to consider when writing a book review.

- What is the book about?
    What is the basic subject of this book?
    Is there one part of the book that seems really important?

- What is the book's theme or message?
    Why do you think the author wrote this book?
    What basic information or message does the author want to share?

- What does the reviewer like about the book?
    Are the characters interesting?
    Does the book contain interesting information?
    Is the information easy to follow?
    Does the book make use of illustrations or other graphics?

page 48

4. Students select a book to review.

Writing

1. After reading the book, students use the form on page 48 to write a rough draft of the review.

2. Students reread the piece to make sure that it makes sense. The writer may seek another person's response.

3. Using the checklist on page 6, students revise and edit their work and recopy on another form if necessary.

Name _____

_____
(title)

_____
(author)

_____
(publisher)

1. What is this book about?   (Tell enough about the book to interest others in reading it, but don't give away the whole story.)

_____

_____

_____

_____

2. Why do you think (or not think) it's a book others should read?   (Give specific examples.)

_____

_____

_____

_____

Business letters are usually persuasive. The writer is asking for something, making a complaint, or writing to an official to express an opinion about a situation.

Prepare in Advance

- "Steps to Follow" on page 41, reproduced on an overhead transparency and for individual students
- business letter form on page 50, reproduced on an overhead transparency and for individual students
- business letter writing form on page 51, reproduced for individual students
- revise and edit checklist on page 6, reproduced for individual students
- stationery and envelopes

Prewriting

1. Using the chart on page 41, review the steps students will follow as they do persuasive writing.

2. Use the overhead transparency on page 50 to review the proper form for a business letter.

3. Discuss the types of persuasive letters that may be written and what each type would contain.

   - a letter of request to a person or a company
   - a letter of complaint to a person or a company
   - a letter to an editor or an official

4. Brainstorm to name people to whom students might write a business letter. List these on a chart or chalkboard. In some instances, all students will write to the same person (e.g., requesting someone to come speak to the class, requesting information the whole class needs, making a complaint about something that affects the whole class). Other times, individual students will select a person to write to.

5. Students are assigned to select a person to write to. They think about what they wish to include in the letter.

Writing

1. Students write a rough draft using the form on page 51.

2. Students reread the piece to make sure that it makes sense. The writer may seek another person's response.

3. Students revise and edit their work, and then produce a final copy on stationery.

4. Students address an envelope and mail the letter.

page 41

page 50

page 51

Name _____

A Business Letter
Basic Form

heading

street address

city, state zip code •———— **your address**

month day, year• ———— **date**

inside address

name of person

street address •———— **name and address of person you are writing to**

city, state zip code

salutation

Dear _____• :

body of letter •

_____

_____

_____

_____

_____

_____

Sincerely, • ———— **closing**

_____ • ———— **signature**

> If the letter is typed, skip four lines and type your name. Sign your name in the space between the closing and your typed name.

Name _____

A Business Letter
Practice Form

_____
(house number   street name)

_____
(city, state   zip code)

_____
(month day, year)

_____
(name and title)

_____
(number   street name)

_____
(city, state   zip code)

_____:
(salutation)

_____

_____

_____

_____

_____

_____,
(closing)

_____
(signature)

An editorial contains both the facts about a topic and the writer's opinion about it. As in other persuasive writing, the goal is to convince the reader to think or act as the writer does.

Prepare in Advance

- "Steps to Follow" on page 41, reproduced on an overhead transparency and for individual students

- editorial planning form on page 53, reproduced for individual students

- revise and edit checklist on page 6, reproduced for individual students

Prewriting

page 41

1. Using the chart on page 41, review the steps students will follow as they do persuasive writing.

2. Share examples of editorials from newspapers or magazines. Discuss the types of information they contain. Determine which parts are fact and which parts are the writer's opinion.

3. Look in the local newspaper for ideas to write about. List topics the students have strong feelings about. Determine which items on the list would make good topics for an editorial.

4. Using the form on page 53, students outline the ideas they wish to include in their editorial.

Writing

page 53

1. Using their outlines, students write a rough draft including:

    - a clear statement of the issue

    - their opinion on the issue

    - the purpose of the editorial

    - a list of facts or examples supporting their opinion

    - a concluding statement

2. Students reread the piece to make sure that it makes sense. The writer may seek another person's response.

3. Students revise and edit their work, and then produce a final copy.

Persuasive Writing

An Editorial

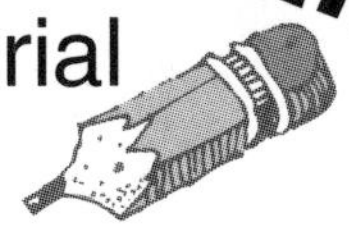

Name ______________________________

1. Clearly state the issue you are writing about. Make your opinion clear in the beginning few sentences.

____

____

____

____

2. State the purpose of your editorial.

____

____

____

____

3. Provide facts and/or examples supporting your purpose.

____

____

____

____

4. Write a concluding statement.

____

____

____

____

____

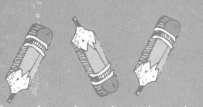

Part V
Writing Reports

What Is It?

Report writing is one of the most common forms of nonfiction writing required of students. Report writing:

- requires a topic narrow enough to cover thoroughly
- poses relevant questions about the topic and answers those questions with relevant facts and examples
- contains information drawn from more than one source
- presents information in an clear, interesting way
- provides graphics to clarify information and to add interest
- includes a bibliography that lists sources

page 55

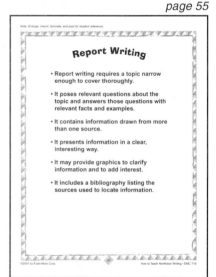

Using This Section

1. Enlarge, mount, and laminate the chart on page 55. Post it on a bulletin board dedicated to nonfiction writing. Use it to introduce report writing, and refer to it as you teach the lessons in this section.

2. This section provides note-taking forms and lessons for writing reports about a person, a place, and an animal. Choose those experiences appropriate to the needs of your students.

3. Three additional types of note-taking forms are provided on pages 65–67. Use these if you wish to do reports on other topics.

page 60

page 64

Before writing reports, students must be able to:
- locate information
- skim to find relevant details
- take notes and summarize information
- write paragraphs containing:
  topic sentences
  supporting details
- write a bibliography

Report Writing

- Report writing requires a topic narrow enough to cover thoroughly.

- It poses relevant questions about the topic and answers those questions with relevant facts and examples.

- It contains information drawn from more than one source.

- It presents information in a clear, interesting way.

- It may provide graphics to clarify information and to add interest.

- It includes a bibliography listing the sources used to locate information.

How to Teach Nonfiction Writing • EMC 719

Name _____

Writing a Report
Steps to Follow

1. Choose a Topic

2. Set up Subtopics

3. Find Information

4. Take Notes

5. Convert Notes to Paragraphs

6. Revise and Edit the Report

7. Produce a Final Copy

8. Add Additional Materials

Bibliography

How to list sources of information.

Book

_____ . _____ .
(last name, first name)   title
author

_____ , _____ .
publisher   copyright date

Magazine

_____ . _____ . _____ ,
(last name, first name)   "title of article"   title of magazine
author

_____ , _____ .
(month year)   page numbers
date

Encyclopedia

_____ . _____ . _____ .
"article name"   title of reference book   year published

Online Sources

_____ . _____ . _____ .
(last name, first name)   (date)   "title of work"
author

_____ (_____)
URL   (date of Web site visit)

How to Teach Nonfiction Writing • EMC 719

Writing a Report
Checklist

Name _____

☐ My topic is: _____

☐ These are the questions I want to answer (subtopics) in my report:

_____

_____

_____

☐ I have read and taken notes in several sources.

☐ I have made a bibliography of my sources.

☐ I have written my rough draft.

☐ I have revised my report—**Content**
    language
    ideas make sense
    story order
    conclusion

☐ I have edited my story—**Mechanics**
    spelling
    punctuation
    capitalization
    grammar

☐ I have copied my final draft.

☐ I have added other materials to my report. (Check those used.)
    ____ diagrams
    ____ illustrations
    ____ maps
    ____ surveys
    ____ graphs
    ____ time lines

A biography is about a real person. It can be a person living today or a person from history.

page 56

Prepare in Advance

- "Steps to Follow" on page 56, reproduced on an overhead transparency and for individual students

- bibliography form on page 57, reproduced on an overhead transparency and for individual students

- report writing checklist on page 58, reproduced for individual students

- note taker on page 60, reproduced for individual students

Prewriting

page 57

1. Using the chart on page 56, discuss the steps students will follow when writing a research report.

2. Work with students to create a list of people they might write about.

3. Brainstorm and list questions the writer should answer as part of the biography.

> Where and when was the person born?
> Where and when did the person die?
> What were the person's early years like?
> What kind of schooling or education did the person have?
> What was interesting and/or important about the person's life?
> Why should the reader be interested in this person?

4. Review the places students can go to find information about the person (books, encyclopedias, interview someone, go online, etc.).

page 58

5. Using the chart on page 57, discuss the formats students should use to list sources of information. Model at least one example for each type of source. Post the models where students may refer to them.

6. Students are assigned or select a person to write about.

Writing

page 60

1. Using the note taker on page 60, students locate and record information about the person.

2. Using the information collected, students write a rough draft.

3. Students reread the piece to make sure that it makes sense. The writer may seek another person's response.

4. Using the checklist on page 58, students revise and edit their work, and then produce a final copy.

Note Taker
Writing About a Person

Name ______________________________

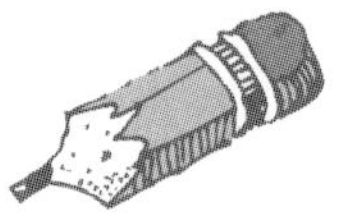

Who (name)

When (he/she lives or lived)

Where (he/she lives or lived)

____
____
____
____
____
____
____

What (he/she does or did)

____
____
____
____
____
____
____

Why (it is important to know about him/her)

____
____
____
____

Students will research and write about an animal.

page 56

Prepare in Advance

- "Steps to Follow" on page 56, reproduced on an overhead transparency and for individual students
- bibliography form on page 57, reproduced on an overhead transparency and for individual students
- report writing checklist on page 58, reproduced for individual students
- note taker on page 62, reproduced for individual students

Prewriting

1. Using the chart on page 56, discuss the steps students will follow when writing a research report.

2. Discuss the animals students might write about. Remind students that it is important to keep the topic narrow or there will be too much to cover in a report—polar bears instead of bears; sharks instead of fish; pelicans instead of birds.

3. Brainstorm and list questions the writer should answer.

> Describe the animal's physical appearance and adaptations.
> Where does the animal live? Describe the animal's habitat.
> Describe its life cycle.
> What does it eat?
> How does it defend itself?
> Think of other interesting and/or important information.

page 57

4. Review the places students can go to find information about animals (books, encyclopedias, interview someone, go online, etc.).

5. Using the chart on page 57, discuss the formats students should use to list sources of information. Model at least one example for each type of source. Post the models where students may refer to them.

6. Students are assigned or select an animal to write about.

page 58

Writing

1. Using the note taker on page 62, students locate and record information about the animal.

2. Using the information collected, students write a rough draft.

3. Students reread the piece to make sure that it makes sense. The writer may seek another person's response.

4. Using the checklist on page 58, students revise and edit their work and then produce a final copy.

page 62

Name _____

Name of Animal: _____

Habitat: _____   Endangered: yes   no

Physical Characteristics:

- _____
- _____
- _____
- _____
- _____
- _____

Special Adaptations:

- _____
- _____
- _____
- _____
- _____
- _____

Habits/Behaviors:

- _____
- _____
- _____
- _____
- _____
- _____

What does it eat?
How does it get its food?

- _____
- _____
- _____
- _____
- _____
- _____

Describe its life cycle.

- _____
- _____
- _____
- _____
- _____
- _____

What are its enemies?
How does it protect itself?

- _____
- _____
- _____
- _____
- _____
- _____

How to Teach Nonfiction Writing • EMC 719

Students will write a report about a place. This may be a place that is part of their own lives, another country, or a place that was important in history.

page 56

Prepare in Advance

- "Steps to Follow" on page 56, reproduced on an overhead transparency and for individual students

- bibliography form on page 57, reproduced on an overhead transparency and for individual students

- report writing checklist on page 58, reproduced for individual students

- note taker on page 64, reproduced for individual students

Prewriting

1. Using the chart on page 56, discuss the steps students will follow when writing a research report.

2. Discuss the types of places students might write about, such as national parks, historical sites, political division (state, country, etc.), or a place that is in the news

3. Brainstorm and list questions the writer should answer.

   What is the name of the place and where is it located?
   What does it look like?
   What happened in this place? or Why is it in the news?
   Do people live there?
   What kinds of plants and animals would you find there?

4. Review the places students can go to find information about places (books, encyclopedias, interview someone, go online, etc.).

5. Using the chart on page 57, discuss the formats students should use to list sources of information. Model at least one example for each type of source. Post the models where students may refer to them.

6. Students are assigned or select a place to write about.

Writing

1. Using the note taker on page 64, students locate and record information about the place.

2. Using the information collected, students write a rough draft.

3. Students reread the piece to make sure that it makes sense. The writer may seek another person's response.

4. Using the checklist on page 58, students revise and edit their work and then produce a final copy.

How to Teach Nonfiction Writing • EMC 719

Name _____

Name of Place: _____

Reason for Name: _____

Geographic location:

_____

_____

_____

_____

_____

_____

Description:

_____

_____

_____

Plants, animals, and/or people living there:

_____

_____

_____

_____

_____

_____

What is its significance? (either to history or today)

_____

_____

_____

_____

_____

_____

_____

Future significance:

_____

_____

_____

_____

_____

_____

_____

How to Teach Nonfiction Writing • EMC 719

Note-Taking Map

Name _____

Topic or Subject _____

Paragraph Main Idea _____

Supporting Information

_____
_____
_____
_____
_____
_____
_____

Paragraph Main Idea _____

Supporting Information

_____
_____
_____
_____
_____
_____
_____

Paragraph Main Idea _____

Supporting Information

_____
_____
_____
_____
_____
_____
_____

How to Teach Nonfiction Writing • EMC 719

Note-Taking
Outline

Name _____

_____
title or heading

I. _____
main idea

   A. _____
detail

      1. _____
information about the detail

      2. _____
more information about the detail

   B. _____
detail

      1. _____
information about the detail

      2. _____
more information about the detail

II. _____
main idea

   A. _____
detail

      1. _____
information about the detail

      2. _____
more information about the detail

   B. _____
detail

      1. _____
information about the detail

      2. _____
more information about the detail

Note-Taking Grid

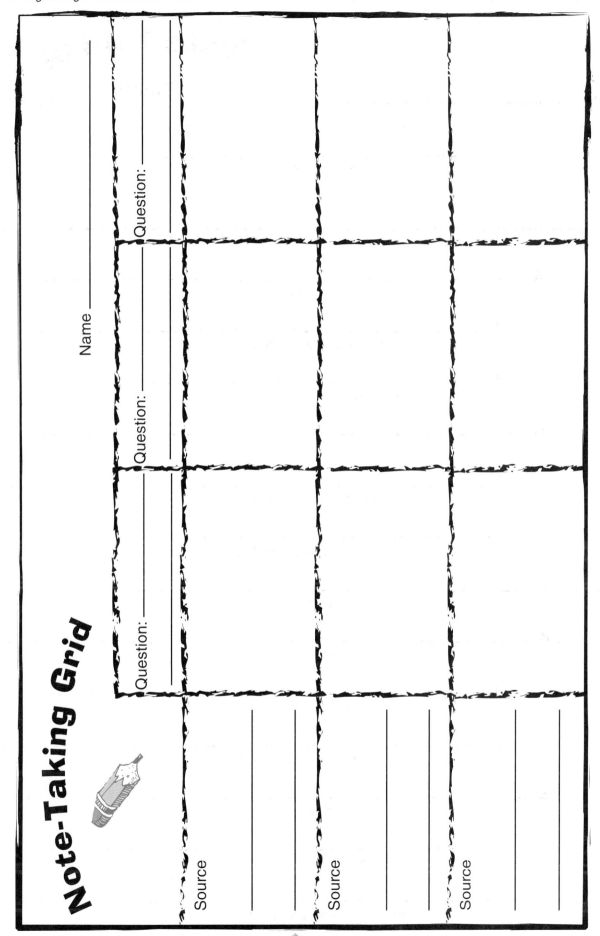

Name _____

Question: _____

Question: _____

Question: _____

Source _____

Source _____

Source _____

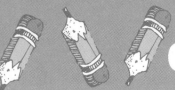

Part VI
Graphic Components

What Are They?

The graphic components of nonfiction writing involve all the symbols and images used to provide added information and clarity to a piece of nonfiction writing. Graphic components include:

- diagrams
- maps
- graphs
- charts
- photographs and illustrations with captions

Using This Section

1. Enlarge, mount, and laminate the chart on page 69. Post it on a bulletin board dedicated to nonfiction writing. Use it to introduce graphic components and refer to it as you teach the lessons in this section.

2. This section provides models and activities for each type of graphic listed above. Choose those appropriate to the needs of your students.

page 69

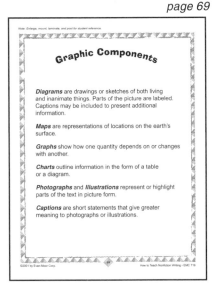

page 71

page 72

page 76

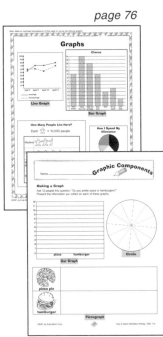

page 77

page 80

page 81

Graphic Components

Diagrams are drawings or sketches of both living and inanimate things. Parts of the picture are labeled. Captions may be included to present additional information.

Maps are representations of locations on the earth's surface.

Graphs show how one quantity depends on or changes with another.

Charts outline information in the form of a table or a diagram.

Photographs and **Illustrations** represent or highlight parts of the text in picture form.

Captions are short statements that give greater meaning to photographs or illustrations.

How to Teach Nonfiction Writing • EMC 719

Teaching the Use of Graphics

Prepare in Advance

- Decide which of the graphic elements you wish to teach. Ideally, you will conduct a lesson on a specific graphic component prior to a writing assignment that would be enhanced by the use of that type of graphic element.

> Diagrams on pages 71–73
>
> Maps on pages 74 and 75
>
> Graphs on pages 76 and 77
>
> Charts on pages 78 and 79
>
> Photographs and illustrations on pages 80–82

- Make an overhead transparency of the model for that graphic element.
- Reproduce the activity sheet(s) for individual students.

Prewriting

1. Use the transparency to talk about the type of graphic being studied. Discuss when and where it might be used. Ask, "How would using a (name type of graphic) be helpful in presenting information?"

2. Have students find additional examples of the graphic element in classroom texts.

3. Review directions students will follow as they complete the activity.

Writing

1. Students complete the activity sheet(s) to practice producing the graphic element.

2. Share and critique the results. Encourage students to use that graphic element in future nonfiction writing activities and in oral presentations.

A picture is worth a million words!

Diagrams

Parts of an Ear

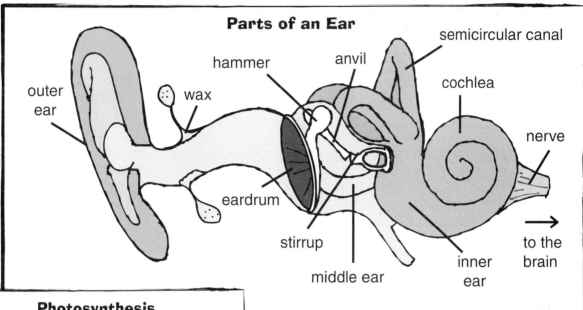

outer ear
wax
hammer
anvil
semicircular canal
cochlea
nerve
eardrum
stirrup
middle ear
inner ear
to the brain

Photosynthesis

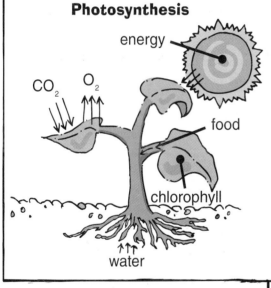

energy
CO_2
O_2
food
chlorophyll
water

Plastic Recycling Process

Plastic is chopped into bits.

The plastic bits are washed and dried.

Plastic is melted and poured into a mold.

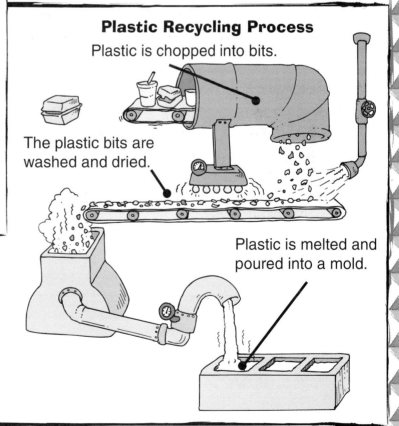

How to Teach Nonfiction Writing • EMC 719

Name _____

Label the Picture

Look at the picture. Write the name of each part on its line.

- monitor
- computer
- keyboard
- mouse

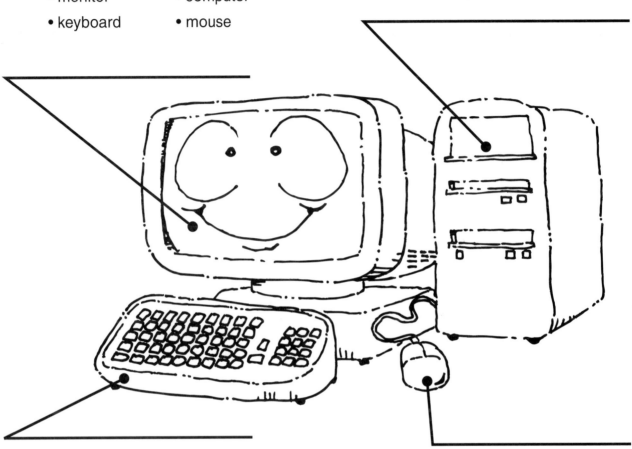

Write a paragraph describing how you use a computer.

_____

_____

_____

_____

_____

Graphic Components

Make a diagram of an object or an animal. Label the parts.

A _____
(kind of object or animal)

Maps

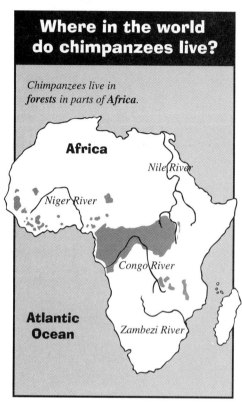

Where in the world do chimpanzees live?

Chimpanzees live in **forests** *in parts of* **Africa.**

Africa

Nile River

Niger River

Congo River

Atlantic Ocean

Zambezi River

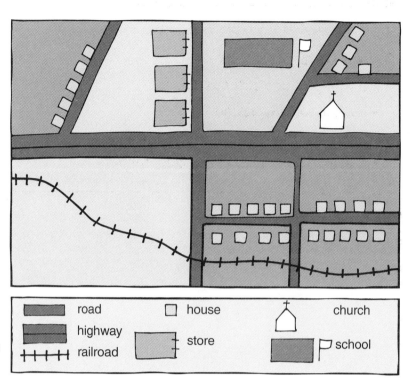

road	house		church
highway	store		school
railroad			

Amusement Park

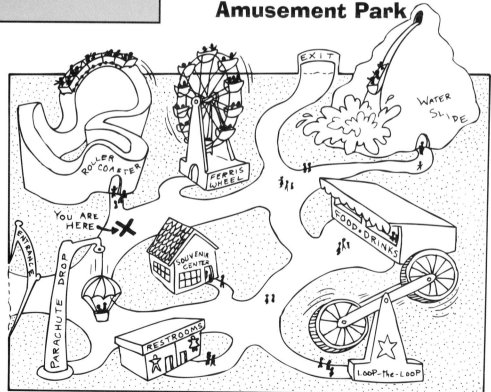

How to Teach Nonfiction Writing • EMC 719

Name _____

Drawing a Map

Make a map of one of these places:

- the school playground
- the route from your house to school
- a map of your favorite amusement park

Graphs

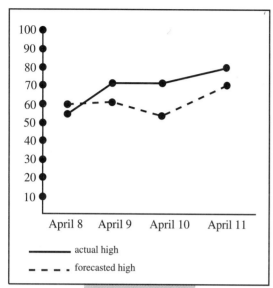

Line Graph

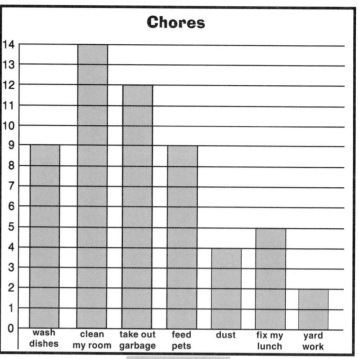

Bar Graph

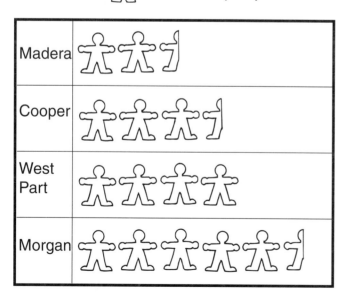

Pictograph

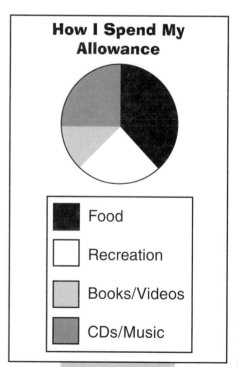

Circle Graph

How to Teach Nonfiction Writing • EMC 719

Making a Graph

Ask 12 people this question: "Do you prefer pizza or hamburgers?"
Present the information you collect on each of these graphs.

12		
11		
10		
9		
8		
7		
6		
5		
4		
3		
2		
1		
0	pizza	hamburger

Bar Graph

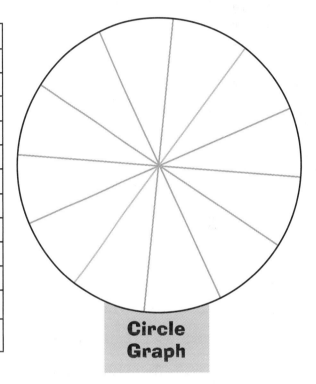

Circle Graph

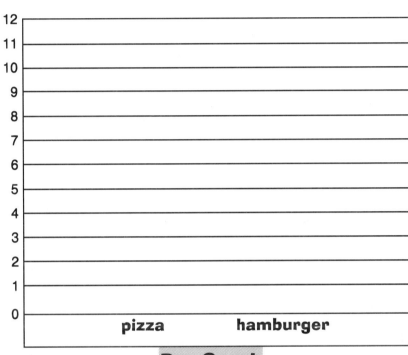

pizza pie

hamburger

Pictograph

Charts

Today's Weather

RAIN

Partly cloudy with a chance of showers on and off all day.

Yesterday

Monterey 69/49, Seaside 71/50

City	Temp	
	Hi	Lo
Austin	75	52
Boston	46	35
Casper	59	22
Chicago	45	36
Dallas	69	45
Fairbanks	32	29
New York	51	39
Portland	66	54
Reno	67	44
Tulsa	66	40
Washington	55	44

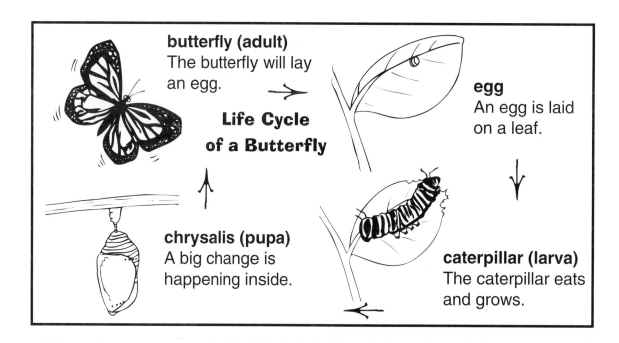

Life Cycle of a Butterfly

butterfly (adult)
The butterfly will lay an egg.

egg
An egg is laid on a leaf.

caterpillar (larva)
The caterpillar eats and grows.

chrysalis (pupa)
A big change is happening inside.

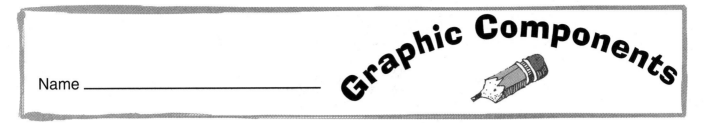
Making a Chart

Find information on one of these topics:

- the sizes of dinosaurs

- the cost of "back-to-school" materials

- the number of miles from your hometown to six vacation places

- wildflowers growing in your home state or province

Take notes here:

On a sheet of blank paper, make a chart to share the information you collected with your class.

Photographs and Illustrations with Captions

Half Dome at Yosemite National Park

Apes come in various sizes...

. . .from the tiny lemur to the large gorilla. The chimpanzee is one of the larger apes.

lemur	**chimpanzee**	**gorilla**
1 $\frac{1}{2}$ feet tall	4 feet tall	5 feet tall
(45.5 cm)	(1.25 meter)	(1.5 meter)

How to Teach Nonfiction Writing • EMC 719

Name _____

Writing Captions

Read the information in this paragraph, and then write a caption for the photograph.

Elephant Babies

An elephant calf is very big. It weighs more than an adult human. The newborn calf sucks milk from its mother. The elephant cow will feed her baby for two years. After a few months of a milk-only diet, the calf will begin to eat plants.

_____

_____

_____

Find a photograph in a newspaper or magazine. Paste the photograph on the back of this page, and then write a caption for it.

Writing Captions

Read the information in this paragraph, and then write a caption for the drawing.

The Midwife Toad

The midwife toad is found in southwestern Europe. The male takes care of the eggs. After the female lays the eggs, the male wraps the strings of eggs around his thighs. Each night he moistens the eggs with pond water or dew. After a month, he takes the eggs to the pond. Tadpoles leave the eggs and swim away.

_____

_____

_____

Draw a picture to illustrate something you like to do. Write a caption under your illustration.

 How to Teach Nonfiction Writing • EMC 719

Part VII
Additional Nonfiction Writing Experiences

Making Lists

Listing can be a preliminary stage to almost any project you do in class. The list can serve as a simple reminder to collect necessary materials before beginning a lesson, as a checklist of steps to follow while creating a multistep project, or a listing of information needed as part of a report.

Application Forms

Occasionally students find they need to fill out an application form (getting a library card, receiving a textbook for class, joining the scouts, joining a sports team, getting permission slips, getting a public bus pass, making a book club order). Take advantage of these opportunities to discuss the importance of accuracy and neatness. If you can get real forms, use them for practice. If not, use the forms provided.

Questionnaires

Questionnaires may ask us to provide our likes and dislikes. They may ask our opinion about a product or an event. They may seek more personal information. A census is a type of questionnaire that asks questions about ethnicity, income, etc.

Announcements

An announcement is a formal notice of something. It may announce a new arrival in a family or a special occasion such as a graduation. It may come through the mail announcing that you have won a prize. It may come from school announcing an open house, a back-to-school night, a class play or concert, or a sports event.

Signs

Signs must present important information in a limited amount of space. They need to be clearly written and large enough to be seen by people walking or riding by. Frequently color or pictures are added to attract attention or present more information. Signs are posted for many reasons: warning signs posted at the sight of a problem or dangerous situation, signs notifying people about an upcoming sale or event, signs about a lost animal or object, and political signs when someone is running for office.

- Lost Pet on page 95
- Vote for Me on page 96

Making Lists
Things I Need to Do Today

Name _____

_____

_____

_____

_____

_____

_____

_____

_____

_____

_____

_____

_____

_____

_____

How to Teach Nonfiction Writing • EMC 719

Name _____

I will need these items to complete my _____ assignment.

1. _____

2. _____

3. _____

4. _____

5. _____

6. _____

7. _____

8. _____

9. _____

10. _____

How to Teach Nonfiction Writing • EMC 719

Name _____

Make a list of topics you find interesting. Add to the list when you think of new ideas. Keep the list in your writing portfolio.

1. _____

2. _____

3. _____

4. _____

5. _____

6. _____

7. _____

8. _____

9. _____

10. _____

11. _____

12. _____

13. _____

14. _____

15. _____

Name _____

When applying for a library card, you will need a parent or guardian's signature and proof that your family lives in the city served by the library.

Fill out the following application for a library card.

Springfield County Library

Please Print

Name _____

           (Last)   (First)   (Middle Initial)

Mailing Address

_____

(Street Address or P.O. Box)

_____

   (City)   (State)   (Zip Code)

Home Address if Different from Mailing Address

_____

(Address)   (City)   (State)   (Zip Code)

I have had a County Library Card before. (Circle)   Yes   No

I agree to follow all the library rules. I will pay promptly any library fines for lost or damaged books. I will be responsible for all materials checked out with my card.

_____

(Signature)

If you are under age 14, your parent or legal guardian must sign this application.

_____

(Signature of parent or guardian)

A job description lets employees know what kinds of work are expected of them. Read the descriptions of three classroom jobs below. Then pick the job you would like to apply for and fill out the application form.

Attendance Monitor

1. Take attendance at 9:00 each morning.

2. Mark *A* for absent students. Mark *T* for tardy students.

3. Take the attendance folder to the office and place it in the basket on the counter.

Equipment Monitor

1. Check balls and jump ropes out at each recess. Check them back in after recess.

2. Rewrite our room number on balls and ropes when the number fades.

Paper Monitor

1. Once a day, pick up papers that are in the teacher's "out" basket.

2. File the papers in student mailboxes.

Job Application

Your name _____

Job name _____

What are your qualifications for doing this job? _____

_____

_____

Why do you want this job? _____

_____

_____

_____

Application Forms
Application for Summer Camp

Camp Summer Fun

Section 1—Personal Information

_____

First Name   Middle Initial   Last Name

_____

Address   City   State   Zip Code

_____

Telephone   Email Address

_____

Date of Birth   Grade   School

Circle: Male   Female

Session You Wish to Attend:

July 5–July 19   July 21–August 6   August 8–August 22

Major Activity:

Sports and Swimming   Computers   Art and Music

Section 2—Emergency Information

1. List any activities the camper cannot participate in _____

2. List any allergies or physical limitations _____

3. List any medications the camper needs to take _____

4. Parent/Guardian's Name _____

5. Work Telephone _____ Home Telephone _____

6. Emergency Contacts

List two people the camp can contact if the parent/guardian is not available.

A. Name _____

Telephone _____

Relationship _____

B. Name _____

Telephone _____

Relationship _____

7. Persons who may pick up the camper besides the parent:

_____

Anyone picking up the child at camp must be listed on this application. Picture identification is required. Please notify the camp director if the camper will be going home with someone other than the parent.

Parent or Guardian's Signature _____ Date _____

A Questionaire
Likes and Dislikes

Name _____ Date _____ Age _____

Check the space that best describes your response.

1. Foods I Eat

Pizza _____ often _____ sometimes _____ never

Hot dogs _____ often _____ sometimes _____ never

Broccoli _____ often _____ sometimes _____ never

My favorite food is _____ .

2. Television I Watch

Cartoons _____ often _____ sometimes _____ never

Sports _____ often _____ sometimes _____ never

News _____ often _____ sometimes _____ never

My favorite television show is _____ .

I watch television _____ hours a week.

3. I Wear Sports Shoes

_____ often _____ sometimes _____ never

The best brand of sports shoe is _____ .

I own a pair of this brand right now.   yes   no

I don't own this brand now, but I plan to buy a pair.   yes   no

Name _____

Announcing _____

Pretend you are going to make an important announcement about an upcoming event that will be presented on television.

Include:

- • a title for the event
- • a description of the event
- • where it will occur (location)
- • when it will occur (time)
- • what it will cost (if there is a cost)

_____

_____

_____

_____

_____

_____

_____

_____

_____

Name _____

An Announcement

Pretend you are writing an announcement for the local newspaper about something special that has happened in your class (the students won a game against the teacher, the class hamster had babies, there's a new pet in class, the teacher got married, you got new computer equipment, etc.).

Include:

- a title
- who or what the announcement is about
- where the event happened
- when the event happened
- why it was memorable or important

_____

_____

_____

_____

_____

_____

_____

_____

_____

_____

Lost Pet

Your pet has disappeared. Create a sign to post around the neighborhood. In as few words as possible, include this information: description of your pet, its name, where it was last seen, any reward being offered, the name and telephone number to call if your pet is found. Include a photograph or drawing of the pet if possible.

Name _____

Vote for Me

You have decided to run for class president. You really want people to vote for you. Create a sign to post around the school that will convince people that you are the person for the job. In a few words, the sign should state the position you are running for, your name, your qualifications for the position, and what you will do for the students if elected. An eye-catching slogan is a good way to capture attention quickly.